AMERICAN ILLUSTRATOR:

ROSE O'NEILL

American Illustrator: Rose O'Neill is part of THE
GREAT HEARTLANDERS SERIES. This collection of
biographies for children describes the lives of local heroes
– men and women of all races and careers – who have
made a lasting contribution to the nation and the world.

AMERICAN ILLUSTRATOR:
Rose O'Neill

Copyright © 2001 by Acorn Books

Acorn Books
7337 Terrace
Kansas City, MO 64114

Cataloguing-in-Publication Data
J.L. Wilkerson
American Illustrator: Rose O'Neill / by J. L. Wilkerson
Library of Congress Control Number: 00-134844
Series Title: The Great Heartlanders Series
ISBN 0-9664470-6-9
1. Rose O'Neill, 1874-1944 - Juvenile literature. 2. Missouri
- Biography - History - Juvenile literature - Commercial Art
- Fine Art - Midwest.

10 9 8 7 6 5 4 3 2 1

Dedication

For all the friends and supporters of THE GREAT HEARTLANDERS SERIES who understand the importance of providing children the opportunity to learn about their local heroes.

Acknowledgements

Thanks to Betty Dixon and Sandy Beaty for their careful attention to detail.

Many thanks to David O'Neill for sharing his knowledge about O'Neill's life and work.

Appreciation to Janelle Ash at the Ralph Foster Museum at the College of the Ozarks, Missouri, and to Lois Holman for their resources.

Gratitude to James Parkison for his research of turn-of-the-century New York City.

Appreciation to Christopher Migneron and John Parkison for their technical help with images.

Book production by Acorn Books, Kansas City, Missouri.

Image Credits:
The Rose O'Neill Foundation, pages v, 4, 10, 26, 66, 82, 102 and 112.
Lois Holman, pages 18 and 88.
Dr. Robert Hendrickson, retired professor, College of the Ozarks, page 117.
Illinois Institute of Technology, page 34.
Lyons Memorial Library, College of the Ozarks, page 74.
National Archives and Records Administration, pages 21 and 22.
All art work by Rose O'Neill is identified. Unidentified illustrations are clipart.

Contents

We succeed in living at all on the terms of this planet by two means, insensibility to facts and sensibility to fancies.
                                                    ~Rose O'Neill

UNDER A MUSHROOM

Rose O'Neill sat under a mushroom. She took a deep breath and smelled the wet, woodsy scent of fallen leaves. A ladybug, as big as Rose's nose, strolled through a nest of leaves. Rose patted its smooth, polka-dot back.

A few feet away a frog sat on a mossy stone. The green, knobby creature made a deep sound, like the trill of two bottom keys on a piano. Its eyes, big as walnuts, blinked at her. Rose blinked back.

A large picture book, opened to the blank pages in the front, was spread across Rose's lap. Rose leaned against the mushroom's stem. With a pencil in one hand, Rose brushed her other hand over the pages, as if carefully preparing them for the touch of the sharp, black lead.

Rose put the pencil to the paper. The paper was cool under the heel of her hand. She took a deep breath and felt the thrill of watching a brand new drawing take life on an empty page. But just as the pencil started to move across the paper, Rose's hand froze.

"The Arts!" a loud voice boomed.

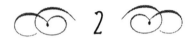

2

UNDER THE TABLE

Suddenly the mushroom disappeared and in its place was a round oak table. The ladybug and frog vanished, too. A teacup and saucepan stood in their places. In an instant, the mossy woods became a kitchen.

From under the O'Neills' kitchen table, Rose saw the legs of her mother and father moving around the room.

"Let me have this child," the loud voice said, "and I will make an experiment. I will teach her the Arts – only the Arts!"

The voice belonged to William Patrick O'Neill, Rose's father. Without seeing him, Rose knew his arms were waving about his head, a grand gesture for his grand words. All of her life – eleven years – this had been Patrick's favorite subject. And Rose loved to hear him talk about the Arts. The way he said the word, Rose knew it must be capitalized.

Rose placed the pencil on the blank page and drew an arching line, exactly matching the humped back of a frog.

"Not only art, Patrick," said Meemie, in a voice as deep and musical as church bells. "Rose needs an ordinary education, too."

Rose sketched the frog's wedge-shaped face and large eyes. She shaded in the eyes, leaving a tiny sliver of white. The drawing trick made the eyes dark but twinkling, like Meemie's.

"Ordinary?" thundered Patrick. Rose saw his feet springing from the floor. The very idea that Meemie would use the name of one of their children and the word "ordinary" in the same sentence caused him to leap into the air in shock and dismay.

Rose sketched the frog's fat legs and its long, tapering toes. They appeared so real that the frog looked as if he might jump from the page. Finally, when every other detail was complete, Rose drew a

Rose drew frogs throughout her life. Here are two that she sketched after she became a professional illustrator.

long line for his mouth, curving the line slightly at the corners so that the frog smiled.

Every day for the last week, Rose had drawn frogs. Frogs swimming…hopping…sitting on lily pads…kissing butterflies. Rose drew them for school friends who loved the funny little creatures with the happy faces.

"She'll need to know that two and two equal four," said Meemie calmly, "just as much as she'll need to know Shakespeare and Michelangelo."

Patrick sighed loudly. "For the life of me," he said, "I can't see why."

⚜

Patrick had always loved the Arts. When he and Meemie began married life in Wilkes Barre, Pennsylvania, he announced that all of his children would excel in one of what he called the Sister Arts – acting, painting, sculpting, drawing and writing.

In Pennsylvania Patrick owned a small bookstore and art gallery. Even the family's home, Emerald Cottage, was filled with fine art and beautiful books. A local Italian artist painted the living room's ceiling with wreaths and cupids.

In 1876, when Rose was two years old, financial troubles forced Patrick to sell the store. He decided to move Meemie and their two children, Hugh and Rose, to the western frontier, near Battle Creek,

5

Nebraska. The O'Neills loaded their covered wagon with fancy furniture, satin drapes and hundreds of books.

Patrick had a grand plan. He would introduce frontier people to the great literature of the world. He would sell them books – beautifully bound books with gold-lettered covers. In his spare time, he would be a farmer.

After the family settled on the homestead, Patrick traveled around Nebraska trying to sell books. But farmers, who struggled daily to earn a living from the land, saw no sense in buying books of poetry, painting and philosophy.

No money came from book selling. And none from farming, either. Farming was a full-time job, not a spare-time one.

When the bank finally repossessed the homestead, the family moved to Omaha, Nebraska. But few people in the town seemed interested in fancy books. For a while Meemie taught school but gave that up after a few months when the family's newest baby became sick.

The O'Neills were always in debt. Almost weekly, butchers, grocers, and landlords knocked at the door trying to collect money for overdue bills.

That morning the grocer came for the weekly payment – now almost a month overdue – and Rose went under the table.

"Mathematics," said Meemie, "is useful for all the arts." Though trained as a musician, Meemie had learned to raise vegetables to help keep her family fed. For there were now three more O'Neill children – Mary Ilena (Lee), James (Jamie) and Callista. Meemie's once delicate fingers had become tough as tree bark. "A little practical knowledge, Patrick, never hurts," Meemie added.

From under the table, Rose drew a large square frame around the frog picture. She watched her mother walk across the room to the piano where her brother Hugh played the musical scales. It was a rented piano. Music, one of the "Sister Arts," Patrick said, was essential to the children's education.

"Lovely, John Hugh," Meemie said, tapping out the rhythm of each note. "Smooth as silk," she said.

"Mathematics has its place," Patrick admitted. "After all, Leonardo da Vinci was an engineer." He tightened the belt of his frayed satin dressing gown and sat on one of the many book piles that filled the room like a forest of crooked stumps. "But nothing must dampen the imagination – no infernal rules to box in the imagination!"

Rose erased the square from around the frog.

A knock at the door sent Meemie

across the room. "Doe, ray, me, fa, so, la, tee, doe," she sang out to Hugh over her shoulder.

From a nearby book pile, Patrick picked up a poetry book by Lord Byron and began to read.

In a few moments, Meemie returned, followed by a large man politely carrying his hat in his hands.

"It's Mr. Moore from the furniture store," Meemie said.

Rose pulled herself further under the table and folded her legs until she was completely hidden from the store owner.

"Ah, Mr. Moore," said Patrick warmly, rising from the book pile to greet the visitor. "So kind of you to favor us with a visit."

"Hello, Mr. O'Neill," said Mr. Moore. He glanced at Patrick's dressing gown and his black slippers. "I've come again about your piano bill. I know it's hard times for you, but it's been over a month since — "

"I'll bet you're a student of Lord Byron," Patrick interrupted. "Am I right, Mr. Moore?" He held the poetry book out for the man to see. And then, without looking at the page, Patrick quoted,

There is a pleasure in the pathless woods,
There is a rapture on the lonely shore,
There is society, where none intrudes,
By the deep sea, and music in its roar:
I love not man the less, but Nature more.

Rose drew a little cluster of flowers near the frog's head.

Mr. Moore insisted that he was not a student of any kind. He said he was a true-blue American citizen. "I don't fancy Lords and Ladies," he said proudly, "and other what-you-call titled folks."

Undaunted, Patrick turned the page of the book and pointed to another poem. He put a friendly arm around Mr. Moore's shoulder and quoted again, this time with even greater passion,

My boat is on the shore,
And my bark is on the sea;
But, before I go, Tom Moore,
Here's a double health to thee!

Here's a sigh to those who love me,
And a smile to those who hate;
And, whatever sky's above me,
Here's a heart for every fate.

Rose drew a heart on the chest of the frog. Using tiny letters, she wrote the word "fate" in the center.

I have Helga but I have

hibicus bush and he telling her all about it. I was told he has seventy variations of his remarks — while the nightingale has one hundred and ninety. I can believe it is the other way.

I loved him to bursting — his lyre and his looks.

Unwithering summer girds me round.

Is St. Petersburg lovelier than this . more stable — less an improbable Arabian night? More actually there?

Are you alive and uttering? The idea of your being there hard by gives articulacy to azure.

Otherwise, I have seen no one to do honour to the blue. There are no brothers to palms — and there's not enough joy for the climate. The pageant goes for little without black eyes and locks, dark gold in the skin and a Latin heart. Do say you're there : and be blest. Rose o'Neill .

of course the right looker-on can be blond as Wotan and still not spoil the scene.

Throughout her life, Rose filled her letters and other writings with imaginative doodles. Rather than scratch through a mistake, Rose drew a little illustration, often wings, as shown here, to cover the mistake.

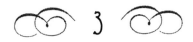

3

THE FORTUNETELLER

Mr. Moore did not favor Lord Byron, nor did he want a copy of Charles Darwin's *The Origin of the Species* as a down payment for the rental fee.

Movers arrived the next day and took the piano away. Over the next few months, it came and went several times, as the fortunes of the family rose and fell. But the unpaid bills increased. Finally the O'Neills had to give up their rented house.

Once again the family packed the wagon and headed off to a new home. There would be many homes – more than a dozen during Rose's childhood in Omaha.

Changes in homes had very little effect on the children's education. Rose and her sisters attended a Catholic school when there was money. Hugh went to Creighton College, a school offering free tuition to boys. When money was short, the girls studied at home, reading from their father's huge library and checking out books at the Omaha library.

Rose was such a familiar patron at the public library that librarians started saving books they knew she would like. Years later, when Rose was an adult, the librarians remembered the O'Neill girl who borrowed all those adult books.

Rose preferred learning at home. At home learning wasn't a separate thing from play or work. Meemie read while she nursed the baby. While Meemie cooked dinner, Patrick etched a portrait of her on a green glass. Instead of just reading Shakespeare's plays, the O'Neill family performed them. Besides learning the poetry of great writers, Rose drew illustrations to accompany her own poems.

Patrick still traveled, sometimes as far as Denver and Chicago, trying to sell his books. On one of his trips, Patrick met a man claiming to be a fortuneteller. Although the man knew nothing of the O'Neills, he said that Patrick had a daughter and then proceeded to describe Rose. This daughter, the fortuneteller said, would some day recover the O'Neill family fortune.

"I told the man I was grooming you for the stage," Patrick told Rose and the others when he returned home. Almost every evening the family performed entertainments – poetry readings, music recitals or theatricals. When Rose showed an interest in playing Ophelia and Juliet and other Shakespearean roles, Patrick decided she should study to become an actress. He paid for her to take singing and elocution lessons. He even found some-one to teach her swimming and diving because he believed performing artists needed physical endur-ance. Like the other O'Neill children, Rose learned to play the piano. She and Meemie gave piano les-sons to earn money for the family.

Patrick continued, "And the fortuneteller said, 'Well, she'll be another Madame Modjeska'."

Helena Modjeska, a Polish immigrant, was one of the most famous actresses in the U.S. Rose had cut out articles in the *Omaha World-Herald* about her perfor-mances in cities across the country.

Helena Modjeska
1844-1909

Rose glanced at her mother, who had hardly looked up from her sewing. Meemie was too practical to believe in fortunetellers. But Patrick told the story with great enthusiasm. He had his heart set on Rose's career in theater. Someday, she might even join the theater company of Edwin Booth, the country's leading Shakespearean actor.

"Why be a Modjeska," Meemie said, and winked at Rose, "when you could be 'The O'Neill'?"

Rose's signature, above, which she used to sign her art work, became famous during the early part of the 20th century.

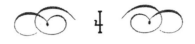

THE O'NEILL
AND THE RED HAND

It was a family legend. The title – "The O'Neill" – was bestowed each generation on the family member who brought distinction to the name. As an educated man who served in Abraham Lincoln's army in the Civil War, Patrick claimed the honored title.

Rose didn't doubt her father's right to the title, despite the poverty and the endless changes of address. He was brave, resourceful and adventurous. Bad luck for him was just an opportunity to tell a good story. He lived his life as a hungry man might eat a ripe apple, savoring each delicious bite. Countless times he called Meemie and the children into the yard to witness a fiery sunset. While Meemie played the piano, he babysat the children, and one time they spent a whole morning watching a spider build an elaborate web across the front door.

Patrick's storytelling was the highlight of many family entertainments. And the story about The

O'Neill and the red hand was the one all the children remembered for the rest of their lives.

A long time ago in Ireland, a leader in the O'Neill family journeyed across the ocean to find a new and distant land for the clan. Other families also wanted to reach this prized land. It was agreed that the first person to lay a hand upon the land could claim it.

The armada of competing ships sailed for many days. A violent storm sent some boats to the bottom of the ocean. After several windless days, when the boats sat still as dead fish on the flat water, many sailors went crazy under the hot sun. Fights broke out, and entire crews perished. But the O'Neill ship moved forward.

One day the journey neared its end. The new land lay on the horizon like the ragged back of a sea monster. Four boats remained in the competition. Only one of them could claim ownership of land.

O'Neill shouted for his crew to hoist the jib. With the additional front sails, the ship sped forward. After a short while, the other boats caught up. Now the four jib booms were neck and neck.

O'Neill called for his crew to throw the food and water barrels overboard. And once again the ship slid ahead of the others. But within minutes, the other boats came alongside. Dozens of barrels littered the wake of the advancing ships.

With the land only a few yards ahead, O'Neill could see tall dark forests and rich green fields. He pulled his sword from the scabbard. He rested his hand on the ship's railing, and with one swift stroke he brought the blade down on his exposed wrist. The severed hand dropped to the deck.

In an instant, O'Neill picked up the bloody hand and threw it onto the shore. In that one mad and gory moment, he won the land for his family. And in that one mad moment he became The O'Neill.

This photograph of Rose's father, William Patrick O'Neill, was taken during the last years of his life. When the family lived in Nebraska, Patrick sometimes worked as a traveling salesman. His homecomings were times of celebration. No matter how unsuccessful the sales trips, Patrick often returned home with presents for everyone. He might bring sheet music for Meemie; a set of chisels for Hugh, who dreamed of becoming a carpenter; paper and pencils for would-be artists, Rose and Lee; a map for studious Jamie; a little account book for Callista, the family manager; and a hand puppet for Clarence, the baby.

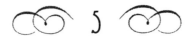

5

EDWIN BOOTH

R ose stared at herself in the mirror. When had she started turning into such a strange looking creature? Other teenage girls didn't look so freakish. She was 13 and the tallest, skinniest girl in her class. Suddenly! The growth spurt seemed to happen over night. One day she was normal, and the next day she looked like a telegraph pole.

Fashionable girls weren't thin, and so Rose draped towels around her waist and tied them with string before putting on her dress. But instead of looking plump, she looked lumpy, as if she had some strange, ribcage disease. To make herself appear short, Rose stooped, and when she sat, she slumped in her chair.

Patrick strongly disliked the stooping and slumping. In large letters, he wrote in charcoal on the kitchen wall:

DON'T BE A HUMBACK.

Of course he had left out the letter "p" in hump-back. Everyone laughed, as Patrick intended. He wanted to encourage Rose, not to break her spirit. Rose was used to adults trying to rally her sinking spirits with humor and sympathy. At the Catholic school, where she was once again enrolled, one of the French nuns praised her art work and encouraged Rose to send a drawing to the *Omaha World Herald*'s art contest for children. "You will win," the nun said brightly. Rose suspected the nun was speaking out of pity.

But Rose did as the nun asked. She sent in a drawing to the newspaper's contest. Sometimes Rose spent the entire day sitting in the middle of her bed, drawing. Piled around her, like a stone wall, were dozens of art and poetry books. Rose imagined that the bed's old quilt was a magic flying carpet, taking her to the lands she read about in the books. As she soared through the sky, she sketched the heroes from epic poems and fantastic legends, including The O'Neill of the red hand.

While drawing, it was easy to forget the freakish body – and *more* freakish clothes. Meemie sewed for the family, although she wasn't very good at it. She almost always had a book in her lap and so her concentration wasn't always on her needle and thread. Buttons often ended up on the wrong side of garments. Right sleeves were stitched to the left armholes. Hems were sewn on the outside of skirts.

Rose also wore used clothes from charity societies. For the rest of her life Rose remembered the embarrassment of going to school in shoes with wrinkled toes and old socks that crumpled around her ankles.

Rose the Telegraph Pole might just as well give up a career in the theater – or maybe she ought to join the circus!

And that was her immediate problem – today she had her first big chance for a stage career. Patrick had arranged for her to meet Edwin Booth. The famous actor was performing in Omaha for a week.

"Don't be a 'humback' in front of Mr. Booth," Patrick said, as they walked out the front door.

Rose promised that she would stand as erect as a soldier. She wore her best dress accented with a black boa – the one she shared with Lee. Also dressed in his best finery, Patrick carried a walking stick with a silver-plated handle.

They arrived at the theater early to see Booth

 perform his most famous role: Hamlet. The tragic story about a prince who is murdered while avenging his father's death was a favorite play of Patrick's.

The slender Booth, who threw himself about the stage like a caged lion, commanded everyone's attention. Sometimes in tears, sometimes in anger, Booth spoke the words of the doomed Hamlet with all the energy of a star athlete.

In the last scene, as Hamlet lay dying of poison, he said goodbye to his friend, Horatio. Rose held her breath, waiting for the famous words.

Clutching his friend's shirt, Hamlet slumped to the ground and gasped, "The rest is silence." And then he died.

Tears ran down Rose's face when she heard Horatio, kneeling over Hamlet's body, speak his lines, "Good night, sweet Prince, and flights of angels sing thee to thy rest!"

As the curtain lowered, Rose clapped until her hands hurt.

Ten minutes later she and Patrick were across the street in a restaurant where Booth was eating a sandwich.

Edwin Booth, shown here playing Hamlet, was a tragic actor whose life was also tragic. His brother, John Wilkes Booth, also an actor, assassinated Pres. Abraham Lincoln in 1865, more than 20 years before Rose met Edwin. The assassin died 12 days later in a barn surrounded by military police. Shamed by his brother's murderous treachery, Edwin retired from the stage but returned at the insistence of his many fans.

Rose was shocked to see the famous actor up close. Years later she described the meeting. Booth's face, she said, was a "beautiful mask of tragedy." His face was a pale yellow and deeply lined. She always thought that his face would resemble one of the smooth-faced statues in her father's Greek Art books. Rose wondered how she would sketch such a face, adding just enough shadow and light to capture the deep-set, intelligent eyes.

Patrick introduced himself and Rose to Booth and explained that his daughter planned to become an actress. Booth nodded slightly at Rose but did not look at her. He went on eating.

Patrick leaned on his walking stick. "I believe my daughter could be talked into reciting a few lines of the great bard."

For the first time, Booth looked squarely at Rose.

Rose's face turned red. The most famous Shakespearean actor in the country was looking at her – Rose Cecil O'Neill, human Telegraph Pole.

"The child is tired," Booth said in his baritone voice. "See, she is about to cry."

As if on cue, tears welled up in Rose's eyes and without thinking she burst out, "The rest is silence."

Booth stared at her in bewilderment. He stood, said he was tired, needed to go to bed. He started to walk out of the room, and then he turned and said, not unkindly, "To play tragedy, you'll have to live a little tragedy."

Rose O'Neill was born in Wilkes Barre, Pennsylvania. When Rose was two years old, the O'Neill family moved to Battle Creek, Nebraska, and later to Omaha, where she began her career as an illustrator. In 1894, the O'Neills settled in Missouri, naming their new home Bonniebrook. Although Rose returned to Bonniebrook for the next 50 years, she mostly worked in New York City. She also lived near Westport, Connecticut, in a mansion she called Castle Carabas.

AN ARTIST'S TEST

Rose won the *Omaha World-Herald* drawing contest. But there was a catch. The editors wanted Rose to come down to the newspaper office.

No other drawing had come close to the skill of Rose's drawing. It looked professional. *Too* professional. Had some adult done it for her? The name of Rose's drawing was suspicious, too: *Temptation Leading Down Into an Abyss*. What 14-year-old child would think of such a sophisticated title?

Rose sat in a straight-backed wooden chair beside the desk of a long-faced man. Several other men stood around the desk. Although she still felt awkward and unattractive, Rose's meeting with Edwin Booth had actually strengthened her confidence rather than weakened it. She had not withered under his piercing gaze, and his puzzling piece of advice had oddly given her hope.

The long-faced man studied Rose's face carefully, as a prospector might who finds a bright

Rose's winning drawing,
"Temptation Leading into the Abyss."

nugget in his pan and wonders if the thing's really gold.

"This drawing is very good," the man said, turning the *Temptation* sketch toward Rose. "Who helped you with it?"

"Helped?" Rose asked. "No one. I did it myself."

"Of course," the man said, his voice full of doubt. "I mean, whose work was it originally...where did you copy it?"

Rose noticed several art books on a nearby desk. Copies of most of the books were in her father's collection at home. The man picked up one of the books.

"Andre Doré," Rose said, recognizing the artist whose works were reproduced in the book.

"Oh, you know the artist," said the man, his eyes widened as if he'd finally trapped Rose. "Did you copy some work by Doré?"

Rose said that, like Doré, she'd found inspiration from Dante's poem, the *Divine Comedy*. She quoted a line from part of the poem called "Inferno":

I came into a place void of all light,
which bellows like the sea in tempest,
when it is combated by warring winds.

Rose pointed to her drawing. "I imagined it would feel like this," she said, "to give yourself up to temptation."

The men looked at each other. Was it possible that a teenage girl could read and understand such a complex poem as the *Divine Comedy*? She was just the daughter of a poor Irish salesman whose large family lived in what people in Omaha called Shantytown.

The man at the desk handed Rose a sketchpad and pencil. "Draw another picture for us," he said.

The men around the desk huddled close to Rose's chair as she began to draw. Her hand turned this way and that, sometimes holding the pencil upright to form solid lines, sometimes letting the

27

lead barely touch the paper to make cross-hatching wisps, and sometimes tilting the pencil on its side to create wide shadows.

As the picture emerged – this time of a woman whose arms were raised prayerfully toward the sky – the men shook their heads in wonder. One man still frowned. He pointed to the figure of the woman.

"Draw more detail in her robe," he said.

Rose laid the pad on the desk and began working on the woman's robe. She knew the man wanted to see the robe's folds, the way cloth drapes over the shoulders and gathers around a belted waist. People always believed that drawing such details was difficult, but Rose had taught herself this technique many years ago when she studied Greek statues and the works of Michelangelo in the books at home.

She handed the finished sketch to the man at the desk. The men stared at the drawing and then at Rose, as if she'd performed a magic trick.

Finally the man sitting at the desk opened a drawer. He took out an envelope and handed it to Rose.

Inside was a certificate. Rose's name was written in a fancy scroll. Under her name was "Best Artist Award." Also in the envelope was a five-dollar gold coin.

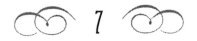

A CAREER IN THE ARTS

The five-dollar gold coin lay on Rose's bed. It fit perfectly inside one of the little squares of the crazy quilt. Spread across the top of the bed, propped up on the pillows, were 20 drawings. Each was as expertly made as the newspaper contest winner.

"The math's simple," Rose said to her father. They both stared down at the coin and the drawings. "If each of the 20 drawings could earn five dollars, then we have – sitting on this very bed – $100."

"There're not that many art contests in the country," Patrick said.

"Not contests," Rose said. "But I could sell them as illustrations to magazines and newspapers." She explained that she had a whole chest full of pictures. For years Rose had studied photographs and engravings in the books in her father's library. She borrowed anatomy and art books from the library. She made endless copies with ink and paper of ancient Greek statues.

"Art isn't about money, Rose," Patrick said, and his usual exuberance disappeared. He looked crestfallen, as if all his and Meemie's efforts to teach her about the Arts had failed.

"But that's why I don't want to be an actress," Rose said. "I'm not good enough." She felt her heart swelling with emotion. "I love to draw. Watching a blank piece of paper come to life – well, there's nothing like it, Papa. It's all I want to do."

In the silence that followed, Patrick stared down at the drawings. For once in his life, he was speechless. Patrick had groomed Rose for the theater. He spent time and money preparing her to become an actress.

And Rose had tried. She even had a bit part in a road show production called *A Pair of Kids*. It was a comedy and Rose's part included sitting mutely on the stage while the lead man ate grapes from her straw hat. The experience was frustrating. The actors were all smiles on stage, but fought like starved tomcats when the curtain dropped. Rose never thought the straw-hat scene was particularly funny. And after 14 performances not even her active imagination could rescue it from foolishness.

Suddenly Patrick's hand shot up like a cavalry officer leading his army to battle.

"The Arts," he said. "Let me have this child, and I will make an experiment. I will teach her the Arts – only the Arts!"

8

ST. REGIS AND THE RAVENS

Rose looked up at the brass knocker in the center of the shiny black door. Above the doorway were an ornately carved crucifix and a brass plaque with the words: The Sisters of St. Regis ~ New York City.

Behind her a milk cart clattered down the brick street. At a nearby grocery, a man and woman, both with thick Irish accents, quarreled over the price of apples displayed in a mountainous heap near the curb.

Patrick had done everything he could to ensure that Rose had what she needed to become an artist. He left brushes and pads of paper in handy spots around the house. He filled cups with freshly sharpened pencils.

He contacted people he'd met during his sales travels – journalists, editors, magazine publishers. For the next five years Rose sold her drawings to western magazines, including Chicago's *Art in Dress* and *Chicago Juvenile* and Denver's *Great*

Inside the illustration:

NEW LAMPS FOR OLD

° ° ° °

TALES FROM THE
ARABIAN NIGHTS
RETOLD . . .
BY . . . .
STANLEY WOOD

ILLUSTRATIONS BY CECIL ROSE O'NEILL

I.

UPON the distant India
shore
Dwelt Mirza in the days
of yore,
The days when magic and its
might
Were both a terror and delight,
The days when Genii came to men,
When spirits peopled glade and glen,
When magic lamps and magic rings
Made poor men rich, and peasants kings;
'Twas in those dear departed days
Which no one speaks of but to praise,
That strange occurrences befell,
Of which I am about to tell.

II.

Now Mirza had a niece, by far
The fairest was Nouronihar
Of any maiden in the court,
Famed for her wit and grace, in short
The fairest lady in the land,
And many gallants sought her hand.
Among these seekers were the sons
Of Mirza, two bold, stalwart ones,
The elder Houssain, Ali next,
And both the lovely lady vexed.
Yes, vexed because it's sad, tho' true,
She found no choice between the two.

Rose's illustration in Great Divide, *September 1893*

Divide. And then Rose and the family decided she should go where she had the best opportunity to learn about drawing and to sell her work – New York City.

With all the street noise, Rose could barely hear the sound of the knocker when she banged it. She set her large carpetbag on the sidewalk and clutched her leather portfolio. It held 60 of her best drawings and was purchased, along with the train ticket, from money received when Meemie sold the family's cow.

It was 1893. Women rarely traveled 1,300 miles alone. Few women worked outside the home, and hardly any woman in the world made a living as an artist.

Rose was about to bang the knocker again when

the door opened. A large nun stood in the opening. Her black cassock blended so completely with the blackness behind her that her round, cheerful face seemed to float bodilessly like a pink balloon in the open doorway.

"Miss O'Neill," she said brightly. "Here you are and not the least bit lost."

Rose spent her first year in New York at the convent. Her goal was to take her 60 drawings around to magazine editors in the hope that they would buy her work. Two nuns accompanied her wherever she went.

On one of her visits to a magazine Rose met a young man named Gray Latham. Gray was trying to get publicity for a movie projector that his father, Woodville Latham, invented. Raised on a southern plantation, aristocratic Gray was popular among the city's high society. He fascinated Rose. Gray described champagne breakfasts in elegant Fifth Avenue drawing rooms and white yachts at Newport, Rhode Island. He seemed perfectly at ease in a city bewilderingly large to Rose. The St. Regis nuns did not forbid Gray to visit Rose, but they insisted on chaperoning the couple.

Rose didn't like it. Everywhere she went, everything she did, she was spied on and followed. What nonsense! She was practically an old woman — nearly 20. After all, Cleopatra ruled Egypt at 17. And Joan of Arc burned at the stake at 19. In her portfolio, Rose carried a novel, full of murder and

On her way to New York, Rose stopped off in Chicago, Illinois. She visited the Columbian World's Fair, which celebrated the 400ᵗʰ anniversary of the discovery of America by Christopher Columbus. The Women's Building (above), designed by architect Sarah G. Hayden, was one of 150 buildings at the fair. Rose saw art work by women from all over the world, including a mural by U.S. painter, Mary Cassatt.

---

gore, about a nunnery. She wrote and illustrated the book while in Nebraska and hoped to sell it to a New York publisher. But the St. Regis convent and its nuns didn't have one ounce of the excitement and adventure of her novel.

Rose sent complaining letters to Meemie and Patrick, who had arranged for her stay at the convent. Rose said she felt like a prisoner. The nuns hovered around her day and night!

Unconvinced, Meemie wrote back, "Pretend they're ravens."

9

EARLY SUCCESS

One day Rose visited *Truth* Magazine. She wore a new dress with plain sleeves and a high collar. She wanted to appear business-like. At her throat was a little green enamel pin in the shape of a four-leaf clover, a lucky charm and a gift from Gray. "Can't hurt," he'd said, when he slipped it into her hand without the nun seeing.

As Rose laid her drawings on the desk, the assistant editor looked across the room at the nuns. They were two of the youngest nuns at the convent. They sat in wide-eyed wonder at the loud clamoring of the magazine office.

"Are you a prisoner?" the assistant editor asked Rose.

Rose knew he was joking, but his reference to "prisoner," her exact word to her mother, surprised her. Certainly the nuns' presence in the magazine office was odd. But the presence of Rose herself was odd, for that matter. The assistant editor only agreed to see Rose because an editor at the *Omaha*

World-Herald, whom the assistant knew, sent a letter of introduction.

Rose looked over at the nuns. Their young faces huddled together against the clamor in the busy magazine office.

"Prisoner? How funny," Rose said breezily, and before she could stop herself she said, "No. They're my sisters. We're such a devoted family. They follow me everywhere."

The assistant editor, staring at the drawings on the desk, barely heard Rose. Luckily, his attention was on the artwork.

No publisher bought Rose's adventure book about the nuns. But within a few months Rose sold almost all of her 60 drawings. She also received assignments to create other illustrations. Rose was young, gifted and determined to succeed. Almost every editor said she had a great imagination.

But art demanded more than imagination. Art that mattered, that touched the heart and soul, demanded a knowledge of life that 19-year-old Rose did not have. Not yet. Booth had said, "To play tragedy, you'll have to live a little tragedy." And, as Rose would discover, he was right.

IN THE WITCH'S HOUSE

During Rose's first year in New York, the O'Neill family moved to the Ozark Mountains. Deep in the hill country of southern Missouri, Patrick bought two little cabins along a creek.

Rose received glowing descriptions of the mountains and hill people. A wild, wooded land, largely unsettled, the Ozarks reminded Meemie of Celtic legends set in enchanted forests. Patrick said the people spoke a colorful language, using words long ago lost to other English-speaking people.

Rose returned to her family shortly before her birthday in 1894. Patrick, Callista and Lee met Rose at the train station in Springfield, Missouri.

Patrick had hired a wagon and driver, named Old Son Stockstill, to take them into the mountains, 50 miles away. Rose later described this journey in detail. Old Son, she wrote, "was chewing tobacco very nicely and spitting neatly into the road. His clothes were ragged and gray as the back of old cedars. He looked as if he had been rained on for years and had got a little mossy."

Patrick climbed up beside the driver. The girls sat on the backbench. Behind the girls were Rose's trunk and drawing board, two barrels, and a crate of chickens. Eager to show her sisters the latest fashion from New York, Rose wore an enormous bell-shaped satin skirt with layers of frilly petticoats. Like a giant pastry, Rose's skirt puffed up around her, taking up half the bench.

Once out of Springfield, the wagon passed miles of farm fields. Wild roses blooming along the fences bordered the green and peaceful blocks of land. It was all very lovely, but where was the wilderness that her family had written about?

Old Son jiggled the reins. In a heavy drawl he called to the two old, slow-moving horses, Buck and Pete, "Buck, you low-lookin' crawlified son of terbacker worm! Scat! Git along!"

Patrick grinned broadly and glanced back at Rose. This was the "language" of the hill people he'd written about. Rose frowned. The language might be quaint, but the man's threats of violence were worrisome.

"Pete, you fly-blown tough-hided onery critter," Old Son continued. "I'll pull up a tree in a minute an' w'ar ye to shoe-strings. If I hadn't come off without my whup unthoughted, I'd have you a-wallopin' along like a skunk out of Kingdom Come."

Neither horse paid the least attention to Old Son's commands. They ambled down the road as if half asleep. Old Son held a limp branch that he rarely swatted at the ambling beasts. Later when he stopped to mend the harness with a piece of string, the two big muzzles leaned into his chest like children used to petting.

Gradually the farm fields disappeared. Little patches of woodland sprouted up like tufts of unruly hair. The ground itself became stony, as knobby as the back of a toad.

By late afternoon, the trees grew closer together, and the land began to pitch and rise. The two old horses strained up and down the tumbling hills. The wagon wound through long tunnels of high-ceiling forests. Low lying branches knocked Rose's hat and pulled out hairpins. Thorny vines, scraping against the wagon, slashed her satin dress.

Old Son looked back at the girls and saw Rose struggling to dodge the vines. The chickens, poking their heads through the crate, pulled the buttons from her skirt. Old Son turned to Patrick, "Be ye really a'threatenin' to carry them pore leetle play-purties down an' lose 'em in the bresh?"

Rose quickly replied, "All I want is just trees, Mr. Son – trees that go on and on. As Emerson said, `All my thoughts are foresters'."

The moon rose. At a break in the trees, Rose saw bluish hills spreading out for miles, their leafy tops silver in the pale light. It was the Ozarks, an ancient mountain range. Her spirits lifted somewhat but she was sleepy and sore from the jolting ride. Her tight corset cut into her. Even the photograph of Gray, which she carried inside her shirt, chafed.

From the hilltop, the wagon descended even deeper into the hilly forest. Rose remembered the stories her family told her about the outlaws who lived in these woods. A few weeks earlier a gang called the Bald Knobbers, organized during the Civil War, had lynched a man. The man had killed his wife and left her body in the cabin. Neighbors found her days later where her children fought off the pigs from the corpse.

The Bald Knobbers put on their cloaks and masks and stole the accused husband from the jail. They hanged him from a tree on the very road the wagon was traveling. Old Son said the man's ghost haunted the hills nearby.

On either side of the road, tree roots twisted around piles of moss-covered rocks. Their giant, contorted forms looked like lurking monsters with slanted foreheads, arched necks and hulking shoulders. At a stream Old Son watered the horses. Their long tails floated in the water, as did the willow branches along the bank. Tree toads trilled and fireflies flickered, like flocks of dancing fairies.

The fifty miles to the O'Neill home could not be made in one trip. Patrick said they would spend the night at the home of a woman named Maw Nabb, who owned two cabins, connected by a rough-hewn passage.

Maw Nabb, with her pointed chin and nose, was, as Rose later wrote, "the witchiest old witch ever found in or out of a fairy tale."

With her corncob pipe, Maw Nabb pointed to one of the cabins. That's where Rose, Calista and Lee would sleep, she said. Patrick and Old Son stayed in the wagon. Maw Nabb, her daughter, Sally, and other members of her family slept in the other cabin.

The girls' feather bed was piled high with colorful patchwork quilts. A fire burning on the hearth warmed the small room against the chill of the dark forest.

Rose slipped her hand under her pillow and felt the photograph of Gray. She fell asleep wondering what he, with his fondness for caviar and diamond cufflinks, would make of these rustic Ozarkians.

In the middle of the night Rose was awakened. Maw Nabb stood in the doorway lighting a candle. She crept across the room. Sally followed on tiptoe. Maw drew near the three sleeping girls. Her sharp face stared down at the bed.

Peering through partially closed eyelids, Rose pretended to sleep. She thought of the Bald Knobbers – murders and late-night lynchings. The frightening tales were coming true. Rose's heart pounded in terror. Would the old woman hear?

Maw raised a gnarled brown hand. It held a long, pointed object. A knife!

Rose drew a long breath and was about to scream when she realized that what seemed to be a knife, now visible in the candlelight, was really the corncob pipe. By that time Maw had turned away from the bed and stood next to the chair piled high with Rose's clothes.

The old woman slipped her pipe into her apron pocket and picked up a pink corset. She and Sally examined the piece of clothing carefully. One at a time, Maw lifted other garments and studied them: a lacy chemise, a plumy hat, a boa, a silk petticoat, an embroidered corset cover and ribbon-trimmed garters.

Maw returned each item to the chair just as she'd found it. And then she turned to the bedside table. She lifted Rose's watch and held it close to her eyes and then showed it to Sally.

"Look, Sal," she said in whispered wonder, "if she ain't got herself a leetle clock!"

11

ENCHANTED FOREST

The next day Rose and the others arrived at the family's homestead. Like Maw Nabb's home, the O'Neills had two cabins linked together by a passageway. Nestled among the hills covered with cedars and ferns, the two small buildings sat beside a spring-fed stream that flowed into Bear Creek.

The family named the place Bonniebrook. And for the first time in her life, Rose believed she had found a permanent home.

Rose and her family felt a strong connection to the hill people. Like the unconventional O'Neills, Ozarkians were unlike the rest of society. After generations of living nearly isolated from the rest of the country, they had created their own unique culture – language, dress and social customs. Almost every weekend, on Friday or Saturday nights, neighbors rode to the schoolhouse for "a literary." The locals called it "a lit'ry," a time for singing, reciting and debating. Ozark men dressed in distinctive outfits. Often with shoulder-length hair, they wore broad-brimmed hats with colorful bands. At dress-up affairs, like a lit'ry, they wore "beauty pins," pieces of colored glass embedded in brass. Their leather belts were wound with ribbons. Boot tops were fringed or cuffed in red leather.

A few days after Rose's arrival a young neighbor began showing up at Bonniebrook. His name was Deary Heathly, whom locals called "the purtiest boy on the crick." Deary arrived unexpectedly, emerging from the forest on his black horse, the color of his own long wavy hair. Because the boy and his horse seemed formed from the same material, the O'Neills called him the Centaur. When Rose told Deary that a Centaur was an ancient Greek creature, half man and half horse, he frowned. He had no time for make-believe things, he said.

Everyone could tell that 19-year-old Deary especially liked Rose. Framed in golden brown hair, her face was smooth as a flower petal. Her eyes twinkled when she laughed and, like all the O'Neills, she laughed often.

Deary would spring out of the woods, claiming that he was after a runaway cow or a lost pig. But he'd hang about the place if he spotted Rose. When he found her drawing, he shyly circled her drawing board with rapt attention. He sometimes stretched out by the creek, sleek and dark as a panther, and watched her.

Once when they sat near each other on a log,

Deary leaned toward Rose and stared into her face. "You're purty as an egg," he said, his blue eyes tearing as if overcome by the sight of her.

And yet there were times when he avoided Rose. If he showed up when she was reading a book or the family was performing one of their theatricals, his face darkened. He turned his black horse around and disappeared into the woods.

Several months after Rose arrived in the Ozarks, Gray Latham came for a visit. He brought with him film he had taken of bullfights in Mexico. He worked for his father's company that was developing a new movie projector. Gray showed the O'Neills the little strips of film he had taken. Everyone excitedly viewed the tiny images through a magnifying glass.

Hill people stared at Gray as though he were a rare, colorful bird. One day at the county post-office, when he tried to mount his horse, the seam of his fancy riding pants ripped out. Locals who saw could not smother their laughter. Gray merely bowed good-naturedly to the spectators and rode off with Rose.

His good nature didn't always prevail. One day he waded up the creek to take a bath. He spread his expensive toiletries – sponge, perfumed soap, colognes, talcum powder, and shaving equipment – on a rocky ledge. He had just soaped his face when he felt a painful sting on his shoulder. Someone hiding in the forest had hit him with a slingshot.

Gray asked Rose if she had fallen in love with any one while they were separated.

"Only a Centaur," she told him.

In fact, she had fallen in love with hill people. She loved the humor and humanity of Old Son, the generosity and curiosity of Maw Nab, and the beauty and passion of Deary.

In 1895 Rose returned to New York. Although she came back to Bonniebrook throughout the next fifty years, she never saw Deary again.

In that half century, Rose became the richest and most famous woman illustrator in American history. Admirers throughout Europe and the U.S. praised her work and sought her company.

But when the clamor of work and the big cities became too much, Rose escaped to the mountains. To a home in an enchanted forest. To a quiet, hidden place, tucked away from the hectic world, where a girl could be "purty as an egg."

12

THAT LITTLE TOUCH OF PITY

Rose sat on a hard bench in the hallway at *Puck* magazine. The young message boy told her the editor would see her at two o'clock.

It was three thirty.

She felt sweat running down her back. It was summer, and she wore a long-sleeve black jacket. *Puck* predominately hired men artists, and so Rose decided that she should look as unfrilly as possible. Gray especially hoped she'd sell her work to *Puck*, probably the most popular magazine in the country. No other magazine paid better.

"Think of the money!" Gray had said enthusiastically. His father's film projector company ran into financial troubles, so Gray found a job selling medical supplies. But he often tagged along when Rose visited magazines.

And Rose *was* thinking of the money. Meemie needed a kitchen at Bonniebrook. Lee wanted tuition for art school. And seven-year-old Clarence (Clink), the youngest O'Neill, outgrew shoes twice

49

a year. For the first time in the family's history, someone had a fairly steady income. That someone was Rose!

On the opposite wall, a clock chimed at the quarter hour. Rose had been waiting for two hours. She told herself to be patient. After all, she knew the editor hadn't forgotten her. Her presence at *Puck* had created a sensation. Considering the number of men who walked past her chair and stared at her — no, gawked at her! — during the last two hours, she suspected that everyone in the building knew she was there.

Rose managed to smile at the parade of *Puck* men, but she didn't feel the least bit jolly. She felt as nervous as an abandoned kitten, left to fend for itself in some dog-infested alley. She felt foolish, too. What if the editor never intended to see her? What if she was left sitting in the hallway merely as a source of amusement for the staff?

One of the passing staff members, a tall, thin man in reading glasses, stopped in front of her. His large, protruding eyes, like boiled onions, peered at her over the tops of his glasses.

"I'm William Gibson," he said.

Rose's heart skipped a beat. She knew perfectly well who he was. He was *Puck*'s art editor, in charge of hiring artists and selecting art for the magazine. Rose was speechless. She expected to see an assistant editor, not Gibson himself.

Rose held up her portfolio and blurted out, "Will you buy my drawings?"

50

"If they're good," he said. The response was so calm and matter-of-fact that it reminded her of Meemie.

A long table, covered in artwork, ran along one wall of Gibson's office. Rose caught her breath when she saw the drawings. They were originals by some of the best illustrators in New York: Frank Nankivell, S. D. Erhardt, Harrison Fisher, Gordon Grant, Stuart Travis and Louis Glackens.

William Gibson pushed aside the art and spread out Rose's drawings. He glanced quickly at each one. She'd included every type of artwork she knew *Puck* used – political cartoons, illustrations for stories, and fancy page borders.

"Where did you go to art school?" he asked, holding up a captioned cartoon titled, `Between Neighbors'."

"Under a mushroom," Rose said, and then was immediately sorry. Gibson would believe she was a smart aleck. Too often she spoke before thinking, but she was self-conscious about her lack of formal training. Other professional artists held degrees from important art schools. The O'Neills never had money enough to send Rose to art school. Everything Rose knew she taught herself.

But Gibson merely shrugged his shoulders, as if her strange comment was something he'd expect from an artist. He said, "I like the way you make the scene funny – so stick to funny."

Did this mean he liked her work? Was he going

51

Rose's "Between Neighbors"
Mrs. Doolan: Did yez hear the landlord had lowered the rint for us,
Mrs. Casey?
Mrs. Casey: Yez don't say! Oi s'pose he thinks he'll lose less money
when yez skip widout payin' it.

---

to buy one of her drawings? Rose tried to ask the questions but stumbled over the words. Gibson said he was not only buying her drawings, he was offering her a job. Full time illustrator for *Puck*.

Years later Rose wrote about this day in her autobiography; she even used it as a scene in one of her published novels. Gibson's last piece of advice remained with her for the rest of her life.

"Remember, stay funny no matter how grim the subject," he said, "but keep that other thing you have – that little touch of pity."

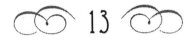

13

A MARRIED, WORKING WOMAN

Rose and Gray Latham were married in 1896, not long after she started to work for *Puck*. Rose found it hard to resist such a passionate admirer. Gray flirted with her all the time. Once at a party, he suddenly raced across a crowded room where Rose was talking to a friend and swept her into an ardent embrace.

Since arriving in New York three years earlier, Rose had succeeded in regularly selling her work. Most artists weren't that lucky. The 22-year-old Rose was the only woman illustrator at one of the nation's leading magazines. And now she was married to one of the city's most eligible bachelors. Her life was full of excitement and romance.

At the *Puck* offices, her fellow artists teased her, especially when she began signing her work "O'Neill Latham." Only Harry Leon Wilson, *Puck*'s leading writer, and William Gibson didn't join the rest in teasing her. They received letters from fans of the new and talented illustrator. Some women

Rose drew this illustration for Puck. *Some people believe she used Gray Latham as the model for the man.*

---

readers thought "O'Neill" was a man because Rose didn't sign her first name to the drawings. They sent her marriage proposals.

Puck's artists drew cartoons and illustrations of people from all parts of American society. Political leaders. High society matrons. Domestic servants. Newly arrived immigrants. The drawings reinforced commonly held attitudes of that time. Women were depicted as helpless, vain or foolish. Poor people and immigrants were shown as ignorant and lazy. Blacks, Jews, and other races and ethnic groups were drawn as stereotypes with exaggerated and unattractive features.

But when Rose sat down at her drawing table she saw Meemie and her sisters in her imagination. She thought of Patrick, an Irish man who was often out of work but was always resourceful and intelligent. She remembered Old Son, Maw Nab and Deary. How could she draw poor people and women without showing their dignity? How could she betray her own life?

Rose's art was different from her fellow artists. The characters she drew were based on real people – people she knew and loved. Her work had, as *Puck*'s art editor, William Gibson, said, "that little touch of pity."

Rose sometimes worked at home, drawing in the little extra room in their apartment. But trying to work when Gray was at home – he often didn't go to work – made concentrating difficult. And besides, their apartment was small. Much of the space was taken up with Gray's belongings. Gray's toiletries covered the dresser top. His clothes filled the wardrobe. Rose's three dresses hung on a hook behind the bedroom door.

Space became even more limited when Woodville Latham, Gray's father, now retired, moved into the extra room.

Rose's income increased with the *Puck* job. She also continued accepting drawing assignments from

This is the cover of Puck's first issue, published in March, 1877.

other magazines. But paying rent and other expenses on just one steady paycheck was difficult. She tried working more hours. Sometimes she sat up until past midnight. Although she was very tired in the morning, Gray made sure she didn't over-sleep. He splashed her with cold water.

Rose knew she could draw as well in Missouri as in New York, and the cost of living wouldn't be as great at Bonniebrook as in the city. When she told Gray about her idea to go to Missouri, he was pleased.

The next day he started planning what he needed to buy in order to live as a country gentleman. He made a list: riding clothes, leather boots, a variety of hats, and fishing gear. He said Rose would need new dresses, too. He made a list for her.

Rose looked at the lists. The cost to buy all those things was so great that Rose gave up her plan to go to Bonniebrook.

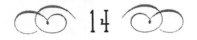

14

A DIFFICULT DECISION

Rose loved her work, but sometimes she felt exhausted from the long hours. She loved Gray, too, but he had very little patience for sending money to Rose's family.

Why should Rose be responsible for all those O'Neills living down in the Ozarks, he asked? Rose tried to explain that she supported her family because they needed the money and she could help. She was making a fine wage. Gray asked why the other O'Neills didn't make their own "fine wage."

On Fridays, Rose visited the magazines that bought her drawings. She dropped off assignments and collected her paychecks. One rainy Friday afternoon, when she stopped at the *Puck* office, the finance department told her Gray had already come by to collect her check. He had left a few minutes earlier.

Rose blushed, but she said nothing. This had happened before. Gray had gone around to *Puck* and the other magazines and picked up her pay-

Rose's cartoon, "The Primrose Path," appeared in Puck *on April 13, 1904.*
Governess: But you must pay attention to the notes.
Flossie: But it's awful hard! I wish mama'd let me learn to play by ear!

---

checks. The money sometimes went to pay Gray's haberdasher, sometimes for theater tickets for them and friends, and once for a new suit for Gray's brother. Frequently, no money remained to send to Missouri.

On this day, however, Rose had no money in her purse, not even enough for bus fare. Now she would have to lug the portfolio a dozen blocks home in the rain.

Harry Leon Wilson stuck his head out of his office. Apparently he guessed the situation, perhaps saw Gray come and go earlier. Rose forced a light-hearted smile and said something about a miscommunication. Harry merely nodded, as if to suggest that he understood. He handed Rose several coins, more than enough to get her home on the bus.

Rose barely noticed the people in the crowded bus. She was making up her mind to leave Gray. At the thought of ending her marriage, her chest actually hurt, as if her heart were being crushed. Rose's reason for leaving wasn't the humiliation she'd felt at the *Puck* office just now. It wasn't the exhaustion from the endless hours of drawing, just to earn enough to pay for Gray's extravagances. It wasn't even the extravagances. It was, however, his utter disregard for her need to support her family.

Her family was important to her. The O'Neills had always worked together – supported each other in whatever way they knew how. Meemie, who once had lovely hands with long, delicate fingers that glided across piano keys like a butterfly, worked so hard that her hands had deep cracks and knobby calluses. Patrick, who was never good at making money, used his many business contacts in Denver and Chicago to help Rose find magazines interested in her art. He had seen to it that Hugh and Jamie had the opportunity to attend Creighton College in Omaha.

Gray and Mr. Latham weren't at the apartment when Rose arrived. She was glad. She packed her belongings, left a note for Gray, and rode across town to a boardinghouse.

The next day Gray showed up at the boarding-house. He danced a little jig in the doorway – something he often did to cheer her up. Rose was delighted to see him. All night she had been miserable. Rose went back to the apartment with him, but not before he agreed that she could send weekly payments to Bonniebrook. She also insisted that money be sent so that Lee and Callista could come to New York where Lee would study art and little Callista could stay for a visit.

Gray agreed, and for a while the situation improved. Lee was enrolled in a New York art school. Callista became a helpful companion to Rose, keeping the apartment tidy and organizing the art supplies.

But the agreement soon fell apart when Gray again started collecting and spending Rose's paycheck.

Once more Rose packed her things. This time she didn't go to a boardinghouse. This time she and Callista boarded a train for Missouri.

A few days later, in 1901, she and Patrick climbed into a wagon and drove to Forsyth, the county seat. At the courthouse, Rose filed for divorce.

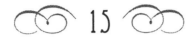

15

THE MONSTERS ARRIVE

The sound of hammering and sawing awakened Rose. It was mid-morning and the builders were back at work on the house. As usual, Rose had fallen asleep in the hammock on the porch.

Bonniebrook had grown. With Rose's money and with the help of local carpenters, the house expanded from two rooms to six. Rose and Meemie had plans to make it even bigger – 15 rooms and three stories when completed.

Rose's oldest brother, Hugh, helped oversee construction. He and Juddy Tittsworth, a young neighbor, were building cabinets and furniture to go in the house. After weeks of woodworking, a fine layer of sawdust covered almost everything in the house and yard.

The entire family was involved in the construction project. Meemie cooked for the building crew, sometimes as many as twenty people. Callista, as usual, helped organize and keep track of everything. Twelve-year-old Clink, the youngest O'Neill, brushed sawdust from the family cat. Rose was particularly fond of Clink, who had a mental condition that in later life required him to receive institutional care. Rose said he had the sensitivity of a poet and was one of the wisest people she ever met. Once when he didn't show up for dinner, Clink explained that the lilacs smelled so powerfully sweet that he hadn't heard Meemie call him.

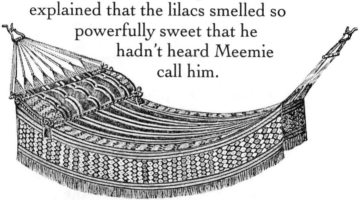

Even Jamie, the studious one, contributed to the building project. In fact, his patient friendliness brought Juddy to the project. Juddy first came to Bonniebrook to chop wood, but he hid behind the woodpile if one of the family came outside. The O'Neills were boisterous and outgoing, a bit overpowering for someone as shy as Juddy. Meemie left his money on a stump, and when he was sure no one would see him, he collected it. In time Jamie coaxed him inside the house and finally into learning woodworking from Hugh.

Rose spent most of the day drawing for *Puck* and other magazines. She had dropped the name

"Latham" from the signature on her drawings. But the thought of giving up on Gray and their marriage was so painful that for a while she continued to write a lone "L" after "O'Neill." She had been miserable since the trip to Forsyth. She hardly slept.

Lately, she began to sign all her work, "Rose O'Neill," making the R, N and two Ls into long, flowing lines. Gibson, *Puck*'s art editor, wrote her that readers, eager to learn the latest about their favorite artist, wanted to know the story behind the changing signatures.

"Curiosity killed the cat," replied Rose, refusing to let her private life become the focus for gossips.

In the afternoon, she rolled up her drawings and put them in mailing pouches. Then she walked down the forested path along Bear Creek and up the hill to Day, the nearest post office. This was the most peaceful part of the day for Rose. She later wrote that in the Ozarks forest she "learned by heart the sound of solitude, the mystical voice made up of winds, flowing water, rustling of leaves and little secret feet; the soliloquies of birds and insects, and the long lament of owls."

One day on her return from Day, Rose reached the top of a hill and heard a rumbling sound. Thunder, she thought. But the sky was soft blue, not a cloud in sight. In the distance, the undulating hills seemed to Rose like the immense muscular arms of construc-

Before 1895 a person viewed a moving picture through a little hole in a machine called a Kinetoscope, invented by Thomas Edison. Woodville Latham, the father of Gray Latham (above), developed a way to project the film onto a wall. On April 21, 1895, in New York City, Gray, his brothers and father demonstrated the Eidolscope, a movie projector they built with the help of W. K. Dickson, who formerly worked for Edison. (Some historians believe Dickson, not Edison, invented the Kinetoscope.) In probably the first movie show in the U.S., a roomful of people watched scenes of boys playing in a park and a man smoking a pipe.

Not long after Rose and Gray divorced, he was murdered in an alley in New York, beaten to death, the authorities believed, by a street gang called the Apaches.

tion workers, rising up as if in joyful praise of the sparkling heavens. Another rumble – and this one followed by a flash of lightning. A wall of black clouds suddenly appeared in the west. Its leading edge boiled over the hills. Within seconds, the sky above was black, pressing down like an iron lid. The once joyful hills now appeared cowering, hunched in terror from the weight of the darkness.

That night, after dinner, when the rest of the family had gone to bed, Rose took out a new sketchpad. She selected a pencil with soft lead so that it would make heavy solid lines. And she began to draw.

At first the figure on the sketchpad was just a dark, flat lump. Through the night Rose switched to hard leaded pencils, then back to soft. Bit by bit the image changed. The figure she drew was round and heavy, unlike anything she had ever done. It didn't look like the slender, attractive people she sketched for story illustrations. It didn't look like the men, women and children she used in her cartoons. The dark form on the paper rose up like a mountain. And almost hidden in the crosshatch of fine lines was a face. The face of a monster.

Just before dawn, Rose closed the sketchpad and put away the pencils. She was exhausted. She fell asleep as soon as she curled up in the hammock. And she would not wake up until morning, with the sounds of hammering and sawing.

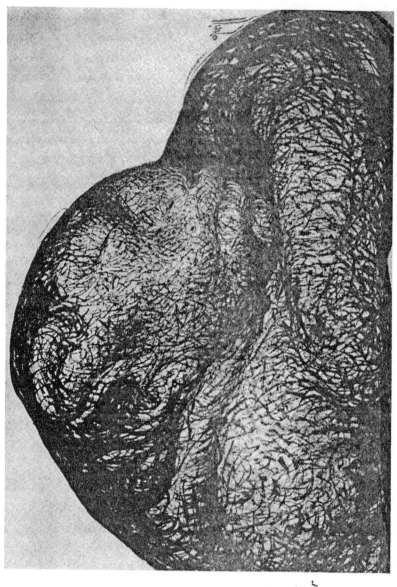

Rose eventually created many monster drawings. She called them her "Sweet Monsters."

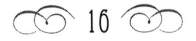

16

MYSTERIOUS LETTERS

One day Callista stood in the yard and called up to Rose who was in the dining room leaning over the drawing board. In the living room Meemie played the violin and Jamie played the piano. Sounds of Beethoven's *Ninth Symphony* drifted through the house like an urgent, threatening storm. Rose peered out the room's new bay window. Callista waved a packet of letters. She had just come back from the Day post office.

"Another letter," Callista called to her sister. "Shall I open it now?"

Rose motioned for Callista to come inside. "Wait until I see the envelope."

In a few moments, the two sisters sat on the window seat, staring down at the newly arrived envelope. In a scrawling handwriting was written

Rose O'Neill
Bonniebrook
Day Post Office
Missouri

No return address. As usual.

Using one of the knives from her cup of art tools, Rose sliced open the envelope. This was the sixth letter she had received. The letters, postmarked New York City, were unsigned. They were love letters.

This letter, like the rest, was chatty. It included news about one of Rose's artist friends. The writer wittily discussed the latest romance novel from a Boston publishing company and a modern art ex-

Rose "was in public ever a sensation; strangers knew instinctively that she must be somebody," Willard Connely, a long-time friend, said. Especially in later years, Rose wore long, flowing robes. "I refuse to box or cage my body," she said. But she was practical, too. When meeting editors or other business people, she dressed conservatively. A celebrity, Rose also wore conservative clothes — regular dresses — when she didn't want to be recognized in public.

hibit at a New York gallery. Any friend might send such a letter to another friend. Only this letter to Rose was unsigned, and it ended with promises to love and cherish her forever.

Rose didn't recognize the handwriting. For several weeks she could only guess at her mysterious suitor. Shortly before she returned to New York in the spring of 1902, she learned his name. It was Harry Leon Wilson, *Puck*'s literary editor.

Gray Latham and Harry were almost complete opposites. While Latham enjoyed the company of high society people, Harry's friends were writers and artists. Harry lacked Latham's good looks. But the literary editor also lacked the younger man's laziness. Harry was a prolific writer, one of the best humorists in New York.

Gray, like Rose, was lively and outgoing. Harry was often somber and quiet. Harry's friends called him "Old Ironface" because his rugged features were often gloomy. Even when Rose and Harry began to date, his gloomy moods came unexpectedly. Sometimes when such a mood struck him, he would walk away, leaving Rose at a beach, park or theater. She had to find her own way home.

When Harry first asked Rose to marry him, she said no. She teased him and suggested that he merely keep sending her letters – unsigned and full of loving promises – and they could go on enjoying each other's company in a way that had made both of them happy.

But Harry persisted, and Rose finally agreed. She certainly enjoyed his witty conversation. They had so much in common. Harry understood her work, encouraged her. He even gave her useful suggestions about a novel she planned to start work on. And Harry greatly valued Rose's opinion about his own work. She was one of the best-read people he had ever met.

After leaving as literary editor of Puck, *Harry Leon Wilson became a successful novelist and playwright. Several of his humorous stories were made into movies, including* Ruggles of Red Gap.

On June 7, 1902, Rose and Harry were married on Long Island, New York. On the ferry coming back, Harry held their marriage license over the railing. He said they didn't need a paper to certify their union. He let the paper fall into the water. Rose watched it bob about on the surface for a few moments. And then it slowly sank.

17

DEATH IN THE FAMILY

Each day a new patch of green came to life in the forest, slowly shedding its drab brown. Bluebells and forget-me-nots broke through a crust of old leaves. Tall junipers sent out tender green shoots at the tips of their old twisted boughs.

This morning Meemie even found a copperhead, dopey from its long winter hibernation, stretched out on the sunny back stoop. With her "snake killing" iron poker, she broke the snake's back with a single whack.

Spring had come to the Ozarks.

Rose and Harry spent their first winter at Bonniebrook. Harry quit his job at *Puck* and began writing a novel. During that winter, Rose also wrote her first novel, *The Loves of Edwy*. She illustrated the two books. When a publisher accepted both books, Rose decided to gather the whole family for a party. There was much to celebrate in the O'Neill household.

Jamie, a gifted student at Creighton College in

Omaha, was applying for a Rhodes Scholarship at Oxford University in England. He was coming home for spring vacation. Rose and Harry talked him into stopping by Columbia, Missouri, where professors at the university could advise him about preparing for the Rhodes entrance examinations.

Callista and Clink were at Bonniebrook. Hugh also lived nearby. He graduated from Creighton a few years earlier, but abandoned plans to go to Harvard in order to marry a local girl. Lee was in art school on the east coast. Patrick was gone, too. Weary of all the noise and bustle from the construction work on the house, he moved to Hemmed-In-Holler, a secluded place in Arkansas. Meemie frequently rode down to visit him.

When Old Son brought Jamie from Springfield, the whole family ran out to welcome him. Clink offered a pair of kittens for Jamie's inspection, and Jamie held out a hand to pat them. The hand shook slightly. Meemie asked if Jamie felt ill. He said he was only tired from the trip. He'd been traveling for three days.

That night at dinner, Jamie said he met a sick woman on the train to Columbia. She was so ill that she shivered with fever. Jamie guided her to a seat and then brought her a drink of water. The other passengers, seeing the feverish woman, took special care to stay away from her.

A worried look came over Meemie's face. Remembering Jamie's pale face earlier in the day, she

asked how he was feeling. He said he was in the "pink of health," and to demonstrate, he skipped up the stairs after dinner, whistling a little tune.

The next morning Jamie was too sick to get out of bed. His neck and back ached, and he had a fever. The doctor came. The news was bad. Jamie had smallpox. Often fatal, the disease was highly infectious.

Jamie feared his illness would keep him too long away from his studies to pass the Rhodes examination. And so Rose read to him. But one day she noticed Jamie's head rocking from side to side. His eyes filled with tears. He couldn't listen any more, he said, couldn't concentrate. Rose wiped his forehead with a cool washrag, and then she left the room.

That was the last time Rose was allowed to visit Jamie. A local woman named Mrs. Snook, immune to smallpox because she survived a mild case of it several years earlier, came to tend the patient. Large bed sheets, dripping with disinfectant, were hung in his room and draped over the stair banisters.

Two weeks after his arrival at Bonniebrook, Jamie became delirious. He talked constantly. Like the cries of a tormented ghost, a stream of senseless words echoed through the house day and night.

Rose and Harry pushed the piano to the bottom of the stairs. They took turns playing. The sound of

the music drifted up to the sick young man, and he was finally quiet.

One evening, the family sat around the living room like mute passengers on a lost ship. Mrs. Snook appeared on the stairway. Rose later recorded the woman's words.

"If there's anybody in the house that knows how to pray," Mrs. Snook said, "let 'em get at it."

Rose went to her studio. She pulled out the sketchbook and began to draw a new monster. This one was kneeling, head bowed, its big hands pushing desperately against an invisible wall, an invisible intruder. Below, in a trembling hand, Rose wrote, "The Fear Outside."

Jamie died that night. Neighbors came and dug a grave by the creek. On a spring day, 16 days after he came home for the last time, Jamie was buried under a blue clump of forget-me-nots.

Rose later wrote about Jamie's death, "Before his death I had felt the family impregnable — like a solid circlet or necklace of stones. Ever since, it has been like a necklace with the string broken. Always a bead might slip off." After Jamie died, Rose donated money to health care organizations in Taney County, Missouri, so that Ozarkians could be vaccinated against small pox.

The drawing at the left is Rose's "The Fear Outside."

This is Bonniebrook in the Ozarks of Missouri. It was Rose's home for almost 50 years. Only two connected cabins were on the land when the family moved here from Nebraska. With Rose's earnings, the 15-room house was built. Her studio was on the third floor. Her balcony is visible in this photograph. Three years after Rose died, the house was completely destroyed by fire. Clink was living alone in the house at the time, but he was not hurt. The house was rebuilt in the 1990s by the Bonniebrook Historical Society.

10

CAPRI

The Isle of Capri sat like a chunk of white marble in the turquoise water. Compared to the dark, mysterious Ozarks, the Italian island was all brightness. For thousands of years, its sun-bleached cliffs attracted writers and artists. Maybe on this gleaming island Rose could forget the terrible loss of Jamie.

Almost immediately after Harry and Rose arrived on the island, Rose met two people who would have enormous influences on her work and life. One was an elderly Civil War veteran, Charles Caryl Coleman. The two remained friends for more than a quarter of a century. Coleman met Rose's father during their service in the Union Army. A landscape painter who was working on a series of paintings of Mt. Vesuvius, Coleman knew everyone on the island.

During one of the many parties at his home, Villa Narcissus, Coleman introduced Rose to

Guillaume Dubufe, the president of Société des Beaux Arts in Paris, France. Dubufe liked Rose's artwork and asked if she would do a portrait of his daughter. Portrait drawing wasn't new to Rose. Almost everyone she knew had inspired one or more of the characters in many of her sketches.

Dubufe was delighted with the finished portrait. He said that it perfectly captured the personality of his little girl. The twinkling eyes revealed her playfulness, and the blond head, tilted slightly as if withdrawing, revealed her shyness. Dubufe suggested that Rose send her work, including her monster drawings – Rose called them her "Sweet Monsters" – for exhibition at the Beaux Arts Salon in Paris.

Harry was glad Rose received the portrait commission and an invitation to exhibit. Maybe the opportunity would lead to something more serious than just pen and ink illustrations.

Harry's work was very serious. They had come to Capri expressly so he could work, undisturbed by the clamor at Bonniebrook or the distractions of New York. But sometimes his gloomy moods would strike, and Harry would remain silent for days. He could not mix work and play, he said. His work demanded his undivided attention. Rose's work was all play. He pointed to the little cherubs adorning many of her commercial art pieces. He said this wasn't serious art.

Rose drew illustrations as well as border art, including all of the artwork on this 1906 Life cover.

But it was exactly those flourishes that made her so popular with magazine editors and readers. Rose had a good sense of decoration and design. If an editor asked her to illustrate a story, she included full-scale pictures as well as "head and tail pieces," also called border art. These were little strips of images (Rose drew playful elves and cherubs) that tumbled along the edges of the pages.

When she first came to New York, her work was timid. Her lines and composition lacked energy. But in the last ten years she had grown in confidence and naturalness. Still eager to learn, she studied the work of other artists, such as the paintings of the

Pre-Raphaelites and the poster art of Toulouse Lautrec. Rose mastered pen and ink, graphite and gouache, pencil and chalk, and watercolor. And most important, her drawings developed a distinctive style – Rose's style – lush, forceful and expansive.

But during this time, a wall was growing between Rose and Harry. Though imaginative people, they needed entirely different conditions to be creative. Harry preferred to work alone without any interruptions. Rose's constant chatter annoyed him. Didn't she know that civilized people didn't even smile before ten o'clock in the morning, much less laugh? Rose called Harry, "Old Ironface." Harry called Rose, "Chucklehead."

They argued often. But quarrels weren't shouting matches. An angry Harry – "Old Ironface" – frequently remained silent for two or three days. He wouldn't even talk to friends who dropped by to visit. And sometimes Harry stormed out, not returning for several days. With each quarrel the wall between them grew taller.

A week after her first exhibit in Paris, Rose learned that the Salon sold all of her work. So popular was her style that Dubufe arranged for an exhibition at Paris' Société des Beaux Arts. The Societe wanted to show all of her work – drawings, paintings and illustrations.

A few months later, in the spring of 1906, Rose and Harry packed to leave Capri. They were going to Paris. Harry had to do more research and writing. Rose planned to visit the Société des Beaux Arts, where she had been elected as a member. It was an enormous achievement for an American woman. The honor gave her equal status with French artists and meant that for the rest of her life she could exhibit in France without submitting her work to a jury.

Shortly before Rose and Harry left Capri in 1906, Mt. Vesuvius near Naples, Italy, erupted. The great volcano sent out orange sprays of fire and clouds of black ash. The brilliant sky turned dull gray. Rose later wrote that she and Harry watched the billowing smoke by day and the flames at night.

When they crossed to the mainland, Rose and Harry found huge drifts of fine ash in Naples. The raining ash followed them half way to Rome, collecting in hat brims and pockets.

Rose's life, too, darkened. With each mile toward Paris, the wall separating the couple grew insurmountable.

This is one of thousands of Rose's Kewpie drawings. Note the little dog in the lower right corner. That dog appeared in many Kewpie illustrations. It is modeled after a bulldog named Sprangel that Rose and Harry owned. Note, too, her playful signature in the bottom right corner. [See page 104.]

19

KEWPIES

Rose shook out the contents of the big envelope. A shower of small strips of paper floated onto her studio worktable. It was her artwork, the head and tail pieces she'd created for dozens of magazines through the years. There were more than a hundred.

A letter fell from the envelope, too.

"What does it say?" asked Callista, standing beside Rose. The two had recently returned to Missouri from New York. Rose's mystery novel, *The Lady in the White Veil*, which she had written and illustrated, had been published a few months earlier. In celebration, she had given a big dinner party, inviting all of her friends – poets, publishers, painters and writers. It was the first time she had seen many of her friends since her divorce from Harry.

The envelope was from Edward Bok, editor at the *Ladies' Home Journal*, one of the dozens of magazines currently buying Rose's illustrations.

Callista laid the scattered pieces of paper neatly across the daybed in Rose's studio. All the illustrations were of Rose's cupids.

Rose read the letter and said, "Bok wants me to draw a series of cupids – just cupids."

"For a story? Cupids? Who'd be writing about baby angels?" Callista asked. She didn't know any writer known for cupid stories.

Rose said Bok planned to find someone to write verses for the drawings. "He wants a whole page full of cupids. He'll find someone to write the verses after I finish the drawings."

Callista shrugged her shoulders and said, "I don't see why someone else needs to write them. If you're envisioning a whole page of cupids, then you're the best one to write about them."

Callista was absolutely right. Why shouldn't Rose write her own verses? She had written hundreds of captions for her cartoons. She had written two novels.

Rose sat at her desk and wrote letters to Bok and W. Martin Johnson, another editor at *Ladies Home Journal*. Along the margins she drew cupids. Each had a round little belly and a pudgy face with large, friendly eyes and a pointed topknot for hair. Rose said that the *Journal* didn't need to find a writer. She'd write the verses for the illustrations. She'd create *little* cupids and call them Kewpies. In the series of verses accompanying the drawings, the Kewpies would act as benevolent elves who did

How would it be for the Christmas cover to have a single figure of a Kewpie like the one. Or a on first page of this letter. Or a little row of them — Or a lot of them flying about in funny little attitudes. —

Or talking to a real Baby = Called "Minding the Baby." — or "Secrets." — If you Like any of these ideas I can make you more elaborate sketch. —

Very Sincerely Yours. Rose o'Neill Wilson. —

Address
Day P.O.
Taney Co.,
Mo. June 14th 1909.

The Ladies Home Journal asked Rose to create a drawing with only cupids. Rose came up with several ideas for the new cartoon character. In this letter [the last page is shown here] to Martin Johnson at the Journal, Rose describes some of her ideas.

good deeds in a funny way. Rose wrote:

> *Kewpie – short for cupid – thus*
> *He's shorter than that famous cuss...*
> *...the Kewps' idea*
> *If understood,*
> *Is to make you laugh*
> *While they do good.*

That winter of 1909 Rose devoted herself to creating the series of drawings and verses of the Kewpies. Even when she wasn't sitting at her drawing board, she was thinking – even dreaming – about the Kewpies. She later wrote, "I had a dream about them where they were all doing acrobatic pranks on the coverlet of my bed. One sat in my hand."

The series of Kewpie pages in the *Ladies Home Journal* were an instant success. Readers wanted more Kewpies and their stories. And so Rose created an entire town – called Kewpieville – of the little cherubs.

Rose put them in scenes from all over the world – from the Arctic to the Equator, in castles and cottages, on land and sea. They rode on clouds, swam in pools, sleighed, climbed haystacks, sat under mushrooms. And everywhere they performed acts of kindness, always humorously.

Other magazines asked for drawings of the good-natured Kewpies. Business people contacted Rose, asking if she'd allow them to use images of the Kewpies on their products and in advertisements.

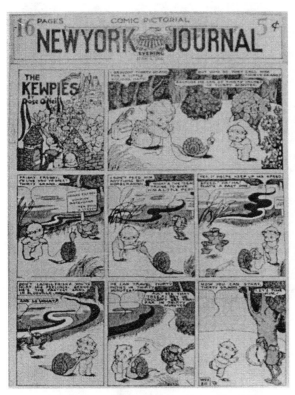

For almost 30 years, Rose created Kewpie illustrations, books and cartoon strips, such as this one that appeared in 1936. The Kewpie character was the most popular cartoon in the history of American culture, until the arrival of Walt Disney's Mickey Mouse.

Before long the fat, little cherubs were printed on almost everything from toys to tools, from fabrics to cans of peas. The Kewpies and their use on commercial products earned Rose a very good income. She was making more money than she'd ever made. The money helped complete the three stories of Bonniebrook. It allowed for Rose's brothers and sisters to go to college and for Lee to attend an art school in Europe.

It was all going so well – and then a Kewpie stepped off the printed page.

Rose's art work and her life challenged tradition, but Rose took criticism good-naturedly. When a few people in the Ozarks disapproved of her red toenail polish, Rose just laughed. She said, "But I love cheerful toes."

20

A KEWPIE TO HOLD

Rose received letters from children all over the world – from New Zealand to New Mexico, from Norway to Canada. Children asked if Rose would make Kewpies they could hold in their hands.

At the same time, toy manufacturers in the U.S. and Europe asked Rose almost the same question. They wanted to use Rose's Kewpie illustration as the model for a doll. Would Rose sell them her idea? In other words would she give permission for them to make Kewpie dolls?

Rose thought for a long time about this. She talked to her friends and family. Rose had two choices: she could sell the Kewpie design to a doll manufacturer for a large sum of money, or she could keep the rights to the design but allow a manufacturer to make Kewpie dolls and pay Rose a

Rose's Kewpie.

percentage – called a royalty – for each doll that was sold.

Rose was already the country's highest paid female illustrator. The biggest magazines and publishers hired her. She drew advertisements for large companies. The idea of all the paperwork involved in keeping track of earnings through royalties didn't appeal to Rose. She was an artist, not an accountant.

But then Callista pointed out that if Rose sold the Kewpies outright then she'd have no control over the final product. What if the Kewpie character that Rose O'Neill made famous on paper didn't look anything like the Kewpie doll that the manufacturer made?

It was that last question that persuaded Rose to accept royalties for the Kewpies. The thought of someone altering her creation in any way made Rose's heart race. No one but Rose must sculpt the final mold for the doll. The doll created from the Kewpie cartoon must look like the Kewpie born in Rose's imagination.

21

THE UGLY DOLL

Rose stared down at the doll. She had never seen anything so ugly. It was the first Kewpie doll from the manufacturer, and Rose hated it. Its puffy shoulders looked more like a boxer's than a baby's. Its round tummy looked bloated, like a water-filled balloon. The face – oh, the face! That was the worst of all. The sly eyes and curved mouth leered up at Rose.

"The thing looks like a fiend," Rose exploded.

Callista had never seen her sister so angry.

During the first two months of 1913, Rose molded and sculpted a Kewpie model. She started by tying rags firmly to a wire framework. Next she mashed plasticine, an oil-based paste, into the folds. She then formed the gray paste into a statuette. Tummy, topknot, wings and smile – every detail was an exact replica of her Kewpie character. Rose made four perfect models. The manufacturers would use the model to create the mold for making the doll.

Rose took one model to the Paris office of the Borgfeldt doll manufacturers. When she unwrapped her model, one of the company officials said, "Take it from me, this little fellow is going to steal the world." The next day the model was sent off to Germany. Copies were to be made, then molds made from the copies.

A happy Rose headed off to Capri to visit Coleman and other friends and to wait for the first doll. Callista, who now lived with Rose in New York, joined her in Italy.

"We'll have to give it up!" Rose stormed, and turned her back on the ugly doll. "They can't make it because they can't *see* it. Obviously they think this outrage looks like the model I gave them. There'll be no doll!"

"Yes, there will," said Callista calmly. She adored and admired her sister more than any person in the world. Rose had conquered every obstacle a woman of that time faced. Rose made a handsome living in a field she loved, in a field mostly denied to women. The fact that Rose made her own – and her large family's – living was amazing enough. But Rose didn't stop there.

Since her second divorce, she'd even rebelled against fashion. A respectable woman had long hair, and if married, she twisted her hair into a bun. A woman also wore a corset. To attain an hourglass-shaped figure, women bound and squeezed themselves into stiff contraptions ringed with whale-

THE
W.H.K & S.
ELLEN TERRY CORSET.

bones. Vital organs and ribs were displaced and compressed, sometimes mutilated. Rose sat at a drawing board for many hours during the day, sometimes late into the night. Why should she wear something so uncomfortable as a corset!

"I don't like harnesses or hairpins," Rose announced when she bobbed her hair.

Callista wrapped up the ugly doll and said to her sister, "We'll go to Germany and see that they are done right."

Rose was grateful for Callista's help. Like Meemie, Callista was practical, believing that most problems had solutions. The next day Rose dashed off a letter to Borgfeldt, telling him not to make another doll until she arrived! Then she and Callista boarded a train in Naples and headed straight toward the heart of Germany.

Eisenach is a tiny town in the Thuringia forest. Surrounded by tall pines, the town reminded Rose of the story of Hansel and Gretel. Johann Sebastian Bach was born in the town. From the balcony of their hotel, Rose and Callista could see Wartburg Castle, where Martin Luther took refuge for eight months. The beds, piled with thick downy quilts, looked like giant turtles to Rose.

An elderly man, gentle and soft-spoken, took Rose and Callista from their hotel to the nearby Borgfeldt factory. Rose held a meeting with the Borgfeldts. She said that she wanted all the molds destroyed, along with a large stock of already manufactured "ogrelings," as Rose called the ugly dolls.

Rose said that she would make 12 models of various sizes. The smallest would be about four inches tall.

Twelve molds from Rose's models were sent to several factories in neighboring villages. Dollmaking was an old art. Generations of Germans — grandfathers, fathers and sons — had worked in the factories. When the smallest doll didn't turn out right, Rose asked that the mold be remade. She was particularly concerned about the small doll. Every detail on its tiny body had to be perfect. These were the dolls, inexpensive because they were so small, that would end up in the hands of poor children. They must be perfect, as good as the big ones. Rose remembered too well the embarrassment of receiving charity offerings as a child in Shantytown.

Each doll was made of unglazed white porcelain, called bisque. After the bisque hardened in the mold, the unfinished doll was put into a container made of fire-resistant clay. The container went into

Rose is painting one of her dolls.

a kiln and cooked at 2,000 degrees Fahrenheit for at least 24 hours.

When cooled, the doll went to the decorating room. After dipping the doll into flesh-colored paint, an artist painted on a yellow topknot, little blue wings and side-glancing eyes, adding the small dab of white to the black iris. Rose painted a sample Kewpie for each decorating room.

The doll then left the painting room and returned to the kiln. The fire set the paint. Rose watched as the pans of dolls slid into the furnace.

Years later Rose remembered this final step: "It was a little bit ghastly to see hundreds of my babies lying white-hot in the great pans."

ROSE OF
WASHINGTON SQUARE

Several thousand Kewpie dolls left the factory that summer of 1913. Within 24 hours after the dolls were first shown in New York, shops and department stores phoned in orders to the Borgfeldt office. Within the month, dolls were shipped across the U.S. Soon people in France, Belgium and other European countries wanted Kewpies. Factory after factory was put at top speed to produce the smiling doll. That fall the company could not keep up with orders.

With the first royalties from the Kewpie doll sales, Rose rented the top floor of an apartment building on Washington Square in New York City. During the ten years that she lived there, she filled the rooms with treasures from her many trips to Europe. Rose's apartment was a favorite hangout for the city's intellectuals and artists.

One day in June, Callista, who lived with Rose, threw a party in celebration of Rose's birthday and the recent publication of *Master-Mistress*, a book of Rose's poems. The studio was crowded with friends. All the "Sister Arts," as Patrick used to say, were represented – poets, dancers, singers, painters, musicians and actors. Kahlil Gibran, a Lebanese poet and painter, read from his new poem, "The Prophet." Violinist Eugene Ysaye, accompanied by Victoria Borscho, a Russian, played the sweetly sorrowful Prelude in E Minor by Frédéric Chopin.

Rose's artist friends, as she wrote in her autobiography, "were all talking people and conversation was the rule of the evenings when the music ceased." That evening the guests talked about a man named John Scopes, a high school teacher in Tennessee, currently on trial for violating the state's ban on teaching Darwin's theory of evolution. For many years, Charles Darwin's theory of man's evolution was a subject of Rose's monster drawings.

The birthday guests sang, "For she's a jolly good fellow," as Callista set down a giant, lighted birthday cake. Written in green icing across the top was "THE O'NEILL." Callista held up a glass of champagne and invited everyone to do the same.

"A toast to Rose –'The O'Neill'," she said, and turned to Rose. "Friend, sister, poet, painter, novelist, illustrator, cartoonist, dollmaker …" Callista laughed and looked around the room. "Have I left anything out?"

"Sculptor," someone said. And it was true. Rose was creating several massive sculptures – one ten feet tall – based on her monster drawings.

Few in the room knew The O'Neill family legend. Rose told the story with as much drama and as many gory descriptions as Patrick had when she was a little girl. The fabric of her velvet caftan, a loose-fitting dress she often wore, fluttered about like the sails of the O'Neill ship.

When the apartment finally emptied, early the next morning, Rose sat at her drawing board. She had work to do. She felt lightheaded by the events of the evening. The praise and congratulations from her friends at the party made Rose feel as if she could tackle a 10-foot block of stone and chisel it into a masterpiece by lunchtime. The evening reminded Rose of the old family entertainments. Nothing gave her more pleasure than the gathering of friends at her home. They were her creative family. She often lent them money and gave them expensive gifts.

And yet during the party Rose overheard someone ask how she had earned the family title, "The O'Neill." She was the wealthiest woman illustrator in the country and the first woman ever elected to New York's Society of Illustrators. When had she ever chopped off her hand – that is, made a personal sacrifice – in order to succeed?

True, thought Rose. Almost from the moment she arrived in New York, art editors wanted to buy her work. She knew she was fortunate. Many artists struggled for years to achieve such success.

Some never achieved it. Consequently, Rose was generous to young artists. At the nearby Brevoort Hotel restaurant, for example, Rose kept a table where anyone who claimed to be an artist could eat a free meal, paid for by Rose.

A critic once called Rose, "a squandered talent." Rose might have been a great artist, the person said, if she had received proper training and hadn't chosen to support her family.

Was that her sacrifice? Had she given up the chance to be called great by art critics in order to help Meemie and the others? Was the loss of that chance like the bloody hand thrown to the shore?

Rose remembered once at Bonniebrook, she and her mother sat on the porch watching her brothers and sisters playing in the yard. "Oh, Meemie," Rose had said, "I love your children!" Both Gray and Harry believed Rose doted on her family too much. It was hard to know. But one thing Rose did know: She would never regret what she had done for love.

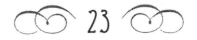

23

A CHANGING WORLD

The Kewpie craze was the biggest success in toy history at that time. Kewpies were the first dolls in history to become popular worldwide. By the early 1920s the Kewpie dolls earned Rose approximately $1.4 million, almost $14.8 million by today's standards.

The success of the Kewpies meant Rose didn't have to work as hard as she once did. In the past, she never said no to an assignment. She always wanted to be sure she had enough money coming in to support herself and her family. Now she could volunteer her time to causes like the women's suffrage movement. In New York and London, she marched in parades, gave speeches, wore placards and made drawings and posters for the cause. In one drawing of a little girl, Rose wrote the caption, "I'm a girl baby, and I'm going to be taxed without representation."

In 1914 war erupted in Europe, but the U.S. did not join the fight until 1917. By then much sentiment had built up in the country against Germany. One anti-German woman threatened to board a ship in New York harbor and smash all the Kewpie dolls in the cargo hold because they had been made in Germany.

German factory workers making Kewpie dolls.

The war was so destructive to German toy-making factories that, by the time the armistice was signed on November 11, 1918, the manufacturing of many toys, including Rose's Kewpie dolls, shifted to the U.S. When Rose visited Germany, she saw that the doll factories lay in ruins, destroyed by bombs. Worse still, many of the workers whom Rose had met during her first visit to Borgfeldt's factory, had been killed in the war.

During the height of her career, Rose lived much of the time in Europe. Her favorite place was Capri, Italy.

These are a few of the signatures Rose used to sign her drawings, especially her Kewpie illustrations and cartoons.

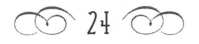

24

CARABAS

Chinko strolled across the veranda. The cat's big belly almost dragged the mossy stones. Lazily, the animal rubbed its back against one leg of Rose's drawing board.

Rose lifted her foot and scratched the cat's marmalade-colored fur with a toenail painted bright red. The stray was one of many adopted by Rose and Callista since they moved from Washington Square.

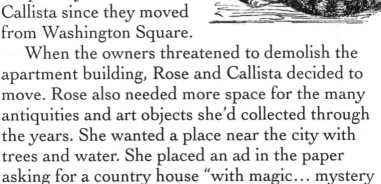

When the owners threatened to demolish the apartment building, Rose and Callista decided to move. Rose also needed more space for the many antiquities and art objects she'd collected through the years. She wanted a place near the city with trees and water. She placed an ad in the paper asking for a country house "with magic… mystery and a touch of terror."

She found such a place in Westport, Connecticut. The house had 11 large rooms and sat on several wooded acres above the Saugatuck River. Rose called it Castle Carabas, the cat's name in *Puss in Boots*.

Rose's friend, Witter Bynner, a writer, was at Carabas for a weekend visit. He held out the day's issue of the *New York Times* for Rose to see.

Several young people lounged around the veranda. Witter didn't recognize any of them. They were more of the hangers-on who followed Rose no matter where she moved. Her generosity was well known. Unpublished authors and would-be artists flocked to her mansion looking for encouragement and a free place to live. Witter and other friends felt Rose was too generous.

Witter handed Rose the art page of the newspaper. The headline said, "Kewpies' Mother Gone Mad." Below was a review of a recent exhibit of Rose's art at the Wildenstein Gallery in New York.

Witter read the review as Rose sketched on her drawing board. The review complained that the exhibit, which included 107 pictures and four sculptures, was a disturbing mix of subjects. Kewpies hung next to Monsters. Smiling mothers cradling babies hung next to tormented amazons. Joy next to terror. Comedy, tragedy. Laughter, madness.

A year earlier the same exhibit appeared at the Galerie Devambez in Paris, and French reviewers praised the unusual combination. The works were "strange and profound," said August Jaccaci, a Frenchman and a consultant for the Metropolitan Museum of Art. He said Rose drew "with the purest line" of any American illustrator.

But American reviewers were harsh. How could the "Mother of the Kewpies" stoop to creating frightening monsters? It was unnatural.

Rose smiled when Witter finished reading. She brushed the heel of her hand across the sheet of paper in front of her and drew a square.

Witter watched the fingers on her right hand. They were twisted from the long years of holding a pen. The swollen calluses looked like the hands of Meemie, who spent 30 years at hard labor until her successful oldest daughter freed the entire family from poverty.

Stroke by stroke the square on the drawing board turned into an ornate box. Its corners curved delicately, and deeply cut jewels encrusted its lid.

When Rose finished, she said, "That's what they want me to climb into. A pretty little box. But I don't fit." Remembering Patrick's words of a long time ago, Rose tapped her head and added, "Nothing must dampen the imagination – no infernal rules to box in the imagination!"

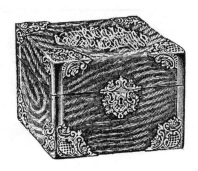

Rose had been poor and rich. She knew the

grief of a beloved brother's death and the joy of working at a career she loved. She felt the misery of two failed marriages and the thrill of the Kewpie doll success. The world was full of contrasts. Life was full of contradictions. Without those combative opposites, life was just a blank piece of paper.

Rose crumpled the drawing paper and rolled it across the veranda. Chinko chased it down the stairs and into the garden.

Rose and her bother, Clink, are pictured here at Bonniebrook. Of all her brothers and sisters, Rose was particularly fond of Clink. Several times during his life Clink required care in mental institutions, which Rose paid for. She also paid for school tuition for her other siblings. Rose's sister, Lee, became a movie scene painter in Hollywood. Callista became Rose's companion and business manager. Hugh lived and worked in Springfield, Missouri.

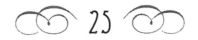

25

OUT OF STYLE - OUT OF WORK

It was the Roaring Twenties. Automobiles filled the streets. Movies were commonplace. Radios crackled with a new sound called Jazz. Women commonly bobbed their hair, as Rose had been doing for a quarter of a century. Hardly anyone wore a corset. Women wore their skirt hems above the knee.

Newspapers and magazines often ran articles about Carabas, calling it an artists' haven. The articles pointed out that a few guests who came for the weekend ended up staying for two years. The press called Rose a "bohemian," an unconventional woman whose easy, cheerful disposition attracted people from all walks of life – from taxi drivers to Pulitzer Prize winners, from concert pianists to fortunetellers. Rose's friends would later say she had a way of making people – no matter how un-happy or ungifted – feel important and hopeful.

And the generosity continued. Rose built a dance studio at Carabas for Ted Shawn where he and Martha Graham practiced. Rose even bought Villa Narcissus from financially troubled Charles Caryl Coleman and paid off the 81-year-old man's $15,000 debt. He could live in the villa for as long as he wanted, she said.

But Rose's income could not sustain this generosity.

Few people on earth had not seen a Kewpie, either a doll or a drawing. But by the early 1930s, doll sales began to decline. In an effort to boost sales, Rose decided to introduce a soft-bodied doll named "Kuddle Kewpie." Rose and Callista opened a Kewpie shop on Madison Avenue in New York. Using a character in the Kewpie cartoon strip, Rose developed a second doll called Scootles. She toured the United States to sell her dolls in department stores.

Rose also tried to sell artwork to magazines and advertisers.

At the turn of the century, Rose helped set the style in commercial art and illustration. But now art editors weren't interested in drawings with fairies and plump babies. Rose told art editors that she could draw any style they wanted, but few were interested.

Rose wrote to her friend, Witter Bynner, "I cannot get jobs. I have not had a story to illustrate (which I used to do every month) from the *Cosmopolitan* for twelve months. Only four other small jobs in a year...The advertisers use photographs...

It is so sickening – telling you these things. I made ten soap advertisements for newspapers but I think the continuation of them was given to a cheaper draftsman. Then I offered to work for less...for anything they wished to pay. Too late."

To make matters worse, the entire country suffered from financial disaster in 1929. The Roaring Twenties ended and the Depression began. Many people, including Rose, had a hard time finding enough work to make a living. In addition to most editors' unwillingness to hire her, Rose's doll business was also declining. And she needed the work. Her family needed money. Clink continued to need medical care. Patrick, who had moved to California, was ill. Meemie often visited him there, but she too was ill.

Friends who came to visit Rose began to notice a change in the Connecticut mansion. The roof leaked, plaster fell from the walls. A potter who had taken up residence in the kitchen had left his clay in the sink, and the drain didn't work.

Finally in April, 1932, Rose made a decision. She later wrote to a friend that she had "come to my senses." With typical twinkle and humor, Rose greeted each Carabas guest one morning with the news of a sad situation. Her long-term guests often ordered food from Mrs. Beers, the local grocer, and charged the bill to Rose. That morning Rose said she needed to protect Mrs. Beer from "the further unfairness of our extravagance." Rose invited all of

Rose's drawing of Meemie, her mother.

them back, however – as long as they brought their own food and linens.

But Rose's fortunes didn't improve. When Patrick died in 1936, she thought seriously of moving permanently to Bonniebrook. He had wanted to stay in California and be buried in the Civil War veterans' graveyard where he could have a cannon fired across his grave.

And then in 1937 news came about Meemie. A telegram urged Rose to come quickly to Bonniebrook. "Mother tells doctor – 'This marathon is about finished'."

26

UNDER A MUSHROOM

Rose closed her eyes. She smelled the wild honeysuckle and heard a frog in the nearby creek. She looked down at the two graves – Meemie and Jamie – marked only by small stones and a bunch of rose buds.

The floor of the Ozarks forest changed with the seasons. Today the wind whirled dirt around a little clump of leaves. In a few months a mushroom would sprout from the leaves. During summer a ground squirrel would make a nest under the leaves. By winter the leaves would decompose into dirt.

Nothing stayed the same. When she was young, that fact was a source of comfort. It meant excitement for a bright future. It meant that beyond these hills she could – and did! – make a name for herself. Her work – her imagination – touched the lives of people all around the world.

Rose was 63 years old, and life's changes weren't

113

always a comfort. Changes meant the death of Meemie and Patrick. They meant the collapse of her fortune. They meant selling treasures she'd collected for years. Friends, who'd known her generosity, tried to help, but many of her old friends were dead. Harry Leon Wilson, hearing of Rose's troubles, sent money. The two had remained friends since their divorce thirty years earlier. But she recently learned that even he was dead.

Atlantic Press asked Rose to write her autobiography and on the last page she wrote:

Few there are who live, alas, —
And they are far from here —
Who know how young and dear I was
When I was young and dear.

After Meemie's death, Rose packed up the contents of Carabas and moved to Bonniebrook. The sale of the old Connecticut mansion, run down from years of disrepair, didn't bring as much money as she hoped.

The newspapers said Rose was retiring. But she wasn't. She could never retire. For one thing, she still loved to draw. But also she needed money. Bonniebrook was an enormous house, always in need of repair. She still had to support Callista and Clink.

Rose brought many of her paintings and statues to Bonniebrook when she left the east coast. She contacted museums in Kansas City and St. Louis, thinking her fellow Missourians would want her art. Galleries in France owned her work. One of her statues, based on a Sweet Monster drawing and commissioned by the city of Oslo, was in Norway. Private collectors in the U.S. and Europe owned her art. But no museum in Rose's home state offered to buy her work.

The students and faculty at the School of the Ozarks, however, were not only interested in Rose's artwork, they were interested in her. At their invitation, Rose gave talks at the school, which was a few miles south of Bonniebrook. In a typically generous act, Rose loaned much of her artwork to the school for display.

Rose is holding a HoHo doll. This photograph was taken shortly before her death.

After she moved back to the Ozarks, Rose sculpted a little doll. A new one called HoHo. It was a seated figure, fat and laughing. But neither the doll nor the autobiography ever came to fruition in Rose's lifetime.

In the last few years

of her life, Rose visited friends around the country. In 1941 she traveled to Sante Fe, New Mexico, to see Witter Bynner. The evening she arrived she suffered a stroke. Although she recovered from the first attack, Rose had other strokes in the next few years.

With her life nearing its end – and it ended on April 6, 1944 when she suffered her last massive stroke – Rose said she knew the place where she wanted to rest forever. It was a small piece of earth in an enchanted forest beside Jamie and Meemie, under a mushroom.

Almost forgotten after her death, Rose and her work were rediscovered in the late 1960s. Today art collectors from around the world, many who are members of the International Rose O'Neill Club, buy her illustrations, cartoons, illustrated books, advertisements, postcards, posters and other work.

Art history scholar, Helen Goodman, wrote, "Rose O'Neill was an American original — as important to the history of illustration, popular culture, and American art as Charles Dana Gibson, Norman Rockwell, or J.C. Leyendecker." Goodman was the guest curator for the 1989 O'Neill art exhibition at Brandywine River Museum, Chadds Ford, Pennsylvania.

In 1997 the University of Missouri Press published Rose O'Neill's autobiography.

J.L. Wilkerson, a native of Kentucky, now lives in Kansas City, Missouri. A former teacher, Wilkerson has worked as a writer and editor for more than 25 years. She is an award-winning writer whose essays and articles have appeared in professional journals and popular magazines in the United States and Great Britain. She is the author of several regional history books. Wilkerson also has written children's books, including other biographies for Acorn Books' The Great Heartlanders Series.

Information about Rose O'Neill's life and times is available through these resources:

Kewpies and Beyond, by Shelley Armitage.

"O'Neill, The Art of Rose O'Neill," an essay by Helen Goodman.

The Story of Rose O'Neill, an Autobiography, edited by Miriam Formanek-Brunell.

Titans and Kewpies, the Life and Art of Rose O'Neill, by Ralph Alan McCanse.

These and other sources were used during the research of *American Illustrator: Rose O'Neill.*

PRAISE FOR
THE GREAT HEARTLANDERS SERIES

"Although the books are clearly designed with an eye toward the classroom...they are well-written and interesting enough to capture children's imaginations on their own."

Omaha World Herald, 10/12/98.

"Acorn Books has launched an outstanding biography series for young readers called 'The Great Heartlanders'."

Midwest Book Review, Children's Watch, 11/98.

"History comes alive in a colorful biography that follows the life of writer Mari Sandoz from her childhood on the Nebraska plains to her last years in New York as a celebrated author...In addition to being a fine biography, the book's account of Sandoz's years as a struggling writer gives the book a universal theme and presents avenues for discussion apart from the historical aspect of the story."

American Library Association, *Booklist*, 2/1/99

"The inviting formats, easy-to-read texts, and black-and-white photographs and sketches will draw both reluctant readers and report writers." *School Library Journal*, 3/99

A Doctor to Her People, "with its maps, drawings, and photographs — some quite charming — packs a fair amount of information into its 100 pages...[Y]oung people who may never have heard of her will be fascinated."

American Library Association, *Booklist*, 6/1/99

OVER FOR MORE REVIEWS

MORE REVIEWS

Curious children will appreciate this well-done book [*A Doctor to Her People*], with its interesting pictures, maps and drawings.

Lincoln Journal Star, 7/11/99

This well-written biography [*From Slave To World-Class Horseman: Tom Bass*] tells the life story of an extraordinary man who was born a slave in Missouri in 1859 and later became known throughout the world as a brilliant horseman...The fast-paced narrative includes a fair amount of fictionalized dialogue. Black-and-white photographs, reproductions, and spot drawings illustrate the text. This is the story of a compassionate man whose genius with horses will be an inspiration to youngsters.

School Library Journal, April, 2000

Frontier Freighter: Alexander Majors is a superb biography and introduction to one of the men who helped shape the American west and is highly recommended for young readers ages 8 - 12.

The Midwest Book Review, "*The Children's Bookwatch*," 7/00

Two new books [*From Slave To World-Class Horseman: Tom Bass* and *Frontier Freighter: Alexander Majors*] are outstanding in their descriptions of dynamic personalities who, by sheer determination and talent, left lasting imprints...With drama and historic detail, Wilkerson pulls youngsters into a world where one man's [Bass's] courage and achievements broke racial barriers long before better-known black athletes Jackie Robinson and Jesse Owens...Details about Majors' personality are especially intriguing."

The Kansas City Star, August 3, 2000

ACORN BOOKS
THE GREAT HEARTLANDERS SERIES

Making history an active part of children's lives.

You can find this book and other Great Heartlanders books at your local fine bookstores.

For information about school rates for books and educational materials in THE GREAT HEARTLANDERS SERIES, contact

Acorn Books
THE GREAT HEARTLANDERS SERIES
7337 Terrace
Kansas City, MO 64114-1256

Other biographies in the series include:

Scribe of the Great Plains: Mari Sandoz
Champion of Arbor Day: J. Sterling Morton
A Doctor to Her People: Dr. Susan LaFlesche Picotte
From Slave To World-Class Horseman: Tom Bass
Frontier Freighter: Alexander Majors
Fighting Statesman: Sen. George Norris
Sad-Faced Clown: Emmett Kelly

Additional educational materials in THE GREAT HEARTLANDERS SERIES are

- ♦ Activities Books ♦ Celebration Kits
- ♦ Maps ♦ "Factoid" Bookmarks
- ♦ Posters

To receive a free Great Heartlanders catalog and a complete list of series books and educational materials, write or call Acorn Books.

Toll Free: 1-888-422-0320+READ (7323)
www.acornbks.com